THE PETROGLYPHS
AT WEDDING ROCKS

AND OTHER POEMS

George B. Moore

Mellen Poetry Press
Lewiston•Queenston•Lampeter

Library of Congress Cataloging-in-Publication Data

Moore, George B. (George Barnard)
    The petroglyphs at wedding rocks : and other poems / George B.
Moore.
        p. cm.
    ISBN 0-7734-2699-X (paper)
    1. Wilderness areas--North America--Poetry. I. Title
PS3563.O6167P48   1997
811'.54--dc21   96-45642
                                                                                        CIP

Cover Drawings by Vern Rutsala

The Edwin Mellen Press   The Edwin Mellen Press
Box 450   Box 67
Lewiston, New York   Queenston, Ontario
USA 14092-0450   CANADA L0S 1L0

The Edwin Mellen Press, Ltd.
Lampeter, Ceredigion, Wales
UNITED KINGDOM SA48 8LT

Printed in the United States of America

CONTENTS

For Vern and Joan,

Mi ritrovai per una selva oscura...
a late night livingroom full of smoke and wisdom

ACKNOWLEDGMENTS

Grateful acknowledgment is made to the following journals where poems from this collection originally appeared.

Hiram Poetry Review:"Sewing the Whale's Mouth Shut"
American Writing: "Wolf"

INTRODUCTION

These poems are wolf-haunted both by actual wolves and, more importantly perhaps, by what wolves represent, the last embodiment of the tragically depleted non-human world. In poem after poem George Moore takes us to the edge of this world in tones that are appropriately somber and elegiac. In some strange way the poems are like his dog—a wolf cross—speaking as they do from our human culture but with one foot always straining toward the primitive. His dog is

> more watchful than those who watch,
> more single-minded than I can ever
> hope to be...
> with the sense of all senses
> at once, the madness of knowing
> too much of what goes on around him.

But the wilderness has been tamed and the wild wolves are compelled to flee

> northward through congested, ailing wilderness,
> skinned by roads, sliced clean, he finds
> no one, no other of his species, no echo of himself.

We no longer see the natural world as the early romantics did—as a refuge and pure source of solace and otherness. For us it is a diminishing thing. Every clearcut along a Western highway reminds us just as do the almost non-existent fish runs and the oil-soaked bodies of birds in the sand. This is our reality and it has changed us. Philip Larkin expresses something of this in his lament, "Going Going," when he says, "I thought it would last my time." But now he knows it won't. And for him, in the early Seventies, "It seem[ed], just now, / To be happening so very fast." Thus we have a new consciousness—the aching sense that the world is finite and that it is disappearing. Especially those parts that are most alien, and therefore most valuable, to us.

But Moore's poems are not simply ecologically right-thinking—though there's certainly nothing wrong with such thought—; these poems run much deeper than that, acknowledging all our guilt, but probing in an effort to enter the true center of the wilderness—the wolf's awareness of the world so totally unlike ours. This is impossible of course but few of us even think of the effort and of the genuine otherness of wild places. Moore is acutely aware of this and his poems move on the thin rind of the primitive world still left us.

Moore feels this sense of otherness in the landscape and most particularly in the haunting wolves. In "Banff Wolves" he says

> I hear the pack at a great distance from the road,
> the song of icy northern air,
> the song of the invisible
> and the ubiquitous,
> the song of an inner part, a hollow
> almost familiar longing.

The wild territory evokes something like a memory, something just beyond reach that finds other counters in these poems in rainforests, other animals—deer, bear, horses—old village sites and artifacts, and the petroglyphs of the title poem which speak out of a buried past without sentimentality when just possibly some accommodation existed between human beings and nature. Sometimes the connection nearly occurs as in "Inside Passage" or in the sense of arts lost and forgotten in "Stone House":

> It is a house of hand formed stones
> that fit together in a way no one knows any longer,
> a craft that passed into the quickness of long days
> and turned walls to impenetrable mysteries.

This also gives some flavor of George Moore's craft—a quiet and subtle language that steadily engages with and sifts the evidence with the sensitivity and integrity that only the true poet is able to bring to our lives. It is language working at its best level, doing what language was intended to do. These remarks only suggest the quality of the book and many other examples could be cited but let me step aside and let you discover the richness of these poems.

Vern Rutsala
Portland 1996

THE PETROGLYPHS AT WEDDING ROCKS

AND OTHER POEMS

WOLF

A gait smooth as current over mossed rock,
but he would wander forever into the unseen
and uncharted, delving through our counterworlds
to the place where he need no longer move.

As he looks at you, his eyes as yellow as fields
of sudden, dusted cinquefoil, the vision
turns back upon itself. Our old movements
are recalled by muscles tightening in the legs.

But his culture is forever changed. And fleeing,
northward through congested, ailing wilderness,
skinned by roads, sliced clean, he finds
no one, no other of his species, no echo of himself.

LAND'S END

Where the land ends
seals sleep
curled against
the crux of the rocks
living between elements
always on this
threshold
at the edge where
the earth is made
and destroyed
between the press
of salt air and rock
osmosis
then raising the great
bulk of their necks
to look out
at a new surface
standing at the door
to the sea

Intruder
marks the sand
at a distance
like a snake
dragging some scepter
of drift wood
trying to claim
what eludes him
sound
in such profusion
white noise
blocking out a sense

of everything
under control
inside or out
looks to where
the seals are staring
without seeing
anything but the sea
at land's end
a place where worlds
fall off a place
that takes him
out

ARCTIC NIGHT

As with a house
that surrounds you and closes off
the outside world from view, congests
the senses, this darkness mingled
like blood with the nerveless cold
shuts off the skin, wraps itself
around the eyes and ears.
For a moment, as evening spread
its depth to a flat white plain,
the winds shut their mouths
and the heart was surrounded
and remembering that hour
how things open out
as body, river, reaches its plain.

CELTIC SEA

I rise up out of the boiling sea
at the foot of a great sandstone mask or head
planted with its face toward the turbulent plain,
and dress for war. The cold eyes watch me
encrust myself with the shields of bronze and skins
like stone—at its threshold, the world
melding between elements of earth
and sea.

I work to anchor myself
to this stone precipice that overlooks the flesh
from where the scream of the wind murmurs
like choir with its voices rising within me
dissipated into the air. It is that particular time
my psychologist says, when to take account
of the impossible solidity of your past
you become invisible to yourself.

Who then arches out over the sea in an arc
of unbearable light, unconscionable purity,
but runs bloody into the sand at his own naked feet?
The metal singes the flesh, relieved
only by the salt air; the tongue of hot sea
lashes my legs momentarily rooted
in the mixture of water and sand
that lifts itself toward wave.

Tacitus tells us how Agricola
standing on the western shore of the northern continent
envisioned the forces that might handily conquer
the last of the Celts. The sea rushed up to him
but would never carry him over,

and now my flesh is a rumor of his horizons,
distant shorelines of rock and rosy spuma,
a stone face and an uncrossed stretch of silky water.

Now, I give back to the sea
the bronze morning, the leathery gusts of my wind.
An older chieftain lies at the mouth of the mask,
eyes looking out toward runic signs
in the human distance. I have come this far by
shear bravado, by dream, past the bloodied feet
of he who stands against the sea, whittled down
by wave and sand, but unconquered.

BANFF WOLVES

East of the Waputik Mountains
the road winds high
through walls of rock and distant perpendicular slopes of evergreen
and more distant snow, and the high edges of thick ice
like an uppermost crust of the world
and the road below, in this crevasse
of wild Bow River
of the Promenade des Glaciers,
seems a temporary thing
a crude hope for a crude sense
of aeonian passage.

East then
up Slate Range, up Boulder Pass
toward Merlin Ridge and Wall of Jericho
at evening, passing
I hear the pack at a great distance from the road,
the song of icy northern air,
the song of the invisible
and the ubiquitous,
the song of an inner past, a hollow
almost familiar longing.

I don't remember now
who I was with,
her face has changed, or disappeared,
a part of this geography as lesson,
a small slide. While a thousand miles north
the snow plains were pushing
toward this silent upheaval.
The wolves were calling to the absence of something in the night
but something was there, at the edge,

returning, a long passage south, something
the road never crossed
and only the thin windlike howl
brings it down through the rock.

LIVING AND DYING IN THE QUINAULT RAINFOREST

It's not that you've not been here.
Perhaps you have.
But my notes confuse me.
Who moves through these images now?
Who carries the old map
that balls with fur in a back pocket?
This living needs a voice:
the rains are famous here,
so much moisture each year that the trees
speak, the fog, a hand
touching their bodies with its language.

Within a mile I'm soaked to the knees
through jeans and boots,
my shirt's stuck to my skin. But then,
the sun is out. The wet tracks
of the long night, morning dew
and broadleaf plants,
slap my legs as I climb
by Irely Creek, through spider webs
outlined in mist. This
is the living:
the slow trudge toward timberline,
the sun caught in among thick wet greens
so that everything explodes
as I pass.

Early enough in May
so no one has disturbed
the notorious owl.
Black bears forget to skirt the trails
after a silent winter.

They look up,
twelve miles from nowhere,
survey the solitary figure
frozen in the moment of his difference
like a red flag on their tundra,
then she and her cubs
climb away.

I stop at each of a thousand streams
to watch the mechanisms of the earth,
the parts that move among themselves
unseen, the tree that at some time
this winter fell,
was caught by others,
old growth holding up the new.
The second day my knees begin to creak,
the insects are out,
the leaves high up have dried.

Kimta Peak, in the distance,
will never be reached;
Above four thousand feet
the snowfields, deep, but in the spring sun
softening, stretch for miles among the rocks;
the trail vanishes between
great walls of hardened drifts.
I climb down to tracks
that cross a wide expanse of snow
wondering who's out here:
great bear prints
jaunt out into the middle, exposed,
as I am. We both turn back,

perhaps a day apart.

I look around at the emptiness
that reaches up to the mountain.
Above the rainforests,
another kind of world, the winds
call out syllables but no names.
I double back at last,
crawl down like an insect
into old growth, the rains
subsiding, the closeness
like a breath in my ear.
The only fear is reaching into spring
before the world has learned
to let you pass. I find a camp
below the bears.

At the edge
of the trees sounds are clearer
than anywhere among the higher peaks
or deeper in the forests. I climb
over redwood blowdown,
walls of fallen giants, but now
the rub of familiar things.
But then the image of those tracks.
The tundra, in blossom,
has reached its fullest limits,
and caught me at the edge
of what I know
and what I know has changed.

OZETTE VILLAGE

Buried beneath five hundred years
of mud and rock, the wet side of a mountain
sliding violently toward the sea,
enclosed the delicate vessels of clay,
the intricate weave, the design of fabrics
seeded the earth, by the sea,
seeded the rift
in the shell of a sleeping world.

In the museum at Neah Bay
I see the remains of the village
encased in glass, in low light,
and hear the screams.
The surf voices rush up at evening
and throw themselves upon the trees
that have fingered their way
up through the ruins
like spear heads
like hairs on a grave.

But there is power here
not mine, a power
held by the feathers and stones, the bones
of some small unknown creature
balanced in the remains
of a lean-to the excavators
abandoned. There is the power of other voices
rattling the needles of the trees
in a dialogue with the riff of surf,
at the sea's dead ends.

What relationship am I

to these nameless bits of things,
the agates of other shores
and microscopic bits of shell
out of unsettled waters,
separated from their pale disguise
of sand and green refuse and volcanic stone
for uses beyond my knowing
for reasons buried,
but buried here?

Shrine or altar, a bench
where others have gathered tokens
of the wind, the museum
miles away and fading
into the right demeanor of interior glows
to capture the primal, or release it.
I hear the five hundred year old screams.
The power of shells, the slashing pulse
of erratic surf. I stand where the mountain was,
where blood talks to the quondam sea.

THE PETROGLYPHS AT WEDDING ROCKS

I lose my sense of direction on an empty strip of coast
twenty miles in from the road, early enough in spring so the crowds
cannot destroy this sense of island, this slow wash of time
in cool days. Then to come upon

the faces carved in black rock, looking out to sea,
or for the sea to look into? Perhaps the first sighting of land after a
    storm,
the sea keyed with the memory of talismans of rock like human anchors.
The day was mist and haze and only slowly cleared, then warmed,

and I had no one to contend with; I saw no ships.
The faces were not alone, but brothered with figures
thin as chiseled sticks, and the rock was hard, lashed by the sea
through centuries of insolence, the slap of salt wash against black stone.

There was a ship carved in the most northerly of the boulders,
a simple vessel with a single sail. Some ancient sighting. Impossible to
    tell
if this crude vessel was the artist's idea of an invader,
some tall mast passing the point five hundred years before,

or if it were his people's craft, an Ozette clan whaling off shore.
The marks, smoothed but deep, the eyes in faces single strokes,
and the weather for the day caught up in lulled reprieve.
I walked among the stones, waisthigh like small monuments

that drew me in. I had not known of them, read no maps,
so ended up on this sandy run without good reason. Now ships pass
further out to sea, the stones wait, their gesture to insure safe passage

lost, or not, faces at the edge of what we see

but cannot know, the signs that link the bodies on the water
to the land, marks that bless activities in danger. Or, another ship
warned off by the artist's wish for isolation, his art a measure
of the cycles, so that his life continues. What these stones see.

THE SEA GIVES UP ITS DEAD

Sometime in the night a sea lion
washed ashore. Its rubbery bulk

adrift in death for how long?
Sea sperm, a living

once nestled in salt skin
and oils, in a thick house of fat.

In the weary fog off
the Northwest coast in early spring

callous gulls pick at her eyes
but the sea will take her back

with tides this evening, but now
a few tourists' kids with sticks

test out the silence
at the long door of death.

I walk toward Canada with fractals
of coastline caught in the mechanisms

of my head, and in the thin dawn
stumble on a dark patch, island, flat

mound of jellied flesh,
a manta ray, surrounded by crabs

that burrow deep at my steps,
sucked up by the wet earth.

The blue gray discus
of its wings, hardened at the tips,

facing back out to sea,
but its eyes too are gone

in death. What death? I see
this thick day like a moist shell

with the insight of its wings
slid ashore in darkness

like an offering. And everywhere
bits of crab where the gulls

have dismembered the dead,
washed ashore like leaves

piled by a storm. Toward Canada
the birds drop down again

to new deposits of old remains,
fight among themselves

for what the sea has left them.
This long gray burial ground

caught in fog, in predawn sounds
of the waves accentuated,

that crash like hands together
and push the bodies up

toward a monument of trees.
Tomorrow's dead are dying now

miles out in the depths,
under the pressure of the rough plain

carried through the artificial
motions of the living

for another day. For the first time
since I was a kid on another coast

I find a starfish, one leg
curled toward its hardened center

its tentacles still soft but drying.
Yet, I cannot keep it. I stand

for a long time staring at its
red blue corpse, at the remnants

of soft suctions on its arms
thinking what would this do

for my desk, on my mantle,
what memory would finally return?

Like a discus, a star
cast out of its spiral by some force

that cannot be called a hand,
some subtle shift in the smallest

pressures of the universe, like that
I spin the starfish back into the sea.

It may and probably will
wash up again, death is always

that complete, full of returns
and feeding the rest on its purest decay,

but that curled arm is here
nestled in the palm of my hand,

sticky with the sand and salt
mixture of the blessing,

a ghost taint, the gesture the earth
made to mark my passage,

to make the fog the physical thought
of the sea full of its ends.

Perhaps these are the eyes
of the manta ray and the sea lion

but I see the starfish moving
long before, when I first wondered

what the sea would do for me
this time, what would be washed up

in its rough test of surf
on the long circle of its shore.

SEWING THE WHALE'S MOUTH SHUT

So that it might not devour the man in the water
who has left his boat, who in the still October air
off Cape Flattery has chosen to enter

the whale's medium, so it does not devour the boat
he sews with a sharpened bit of iron
salvaged from a passing European ship.

A long Ozette needle tied with gut and worked
with a spinner's wide arc as water churns
and the tail listlessly marks the note of a tired heart.

This close to the eye, this angle of the dance
before the end, a trailing in behind the oars
cutting the water, the sewer clings to the unction skin

and works alone, hands and eyes hard to the task
but alert to his movements, watched by one who dies
with others, at the edge of a neighboring, alien world.

INSIDE PASSAGE

Port Hardy Ferry, North, 9:00 a.m.
late in August 1990, and the first thing
is water spouting up from the tail sides,
a giant vortex aimed at the disappearing world.
Fitz Hugh Sound and suddenly
the centuries are dissolvable, indistinguishable
with their long ranges crowed with pine
and the Sound, a narrow passage
back into the vortex of water off the ferry
and standing looking back
toward Vancouver Island
we pass from one world into another
from one time into a time not yet designated
by these human marks, the sight
and sounds of having been there,
a time not yet registered in the crux
of time-space; in shirtsleeves
the channel air is lingering warm
and the noise of the engines
drowning out the incidental noises
of the sky and earth, merging sounds
dovetailed with thoughts, a smooth hum
or rumble, oscillation of low guttural song
sucking us inward, into the land,
into the time that the land has not left,
into the narrows as into the bloodstream
and I try a note, a line from a song
because no one can hear and there is
no one near on the stern,
noise clouding over the light thin sounds
moving toward this other world,
noise making us part of its body, this

fifteen hour passage, making the passage
a trail drawn on water
to here, where I stand, looking back
at the forests darkening, voicing out
almost as if to heal over the human
sound with the more powerful finality
of their silent call,
healing over the ship's thin passage
with a turbulent white scar.

LEAVING WALT WHITMAN

After weeks of the bard's incessant chanting into wind and sea
we leave him, standing on the shore at dusk in the stillness of an earth
more corrupt and yet more complacent. He dreamed we dreamed and
    saw

past the slow crossings of the bay that this day would arrive
somewhere in his busy future, somewhere out among the lives of this
criss-crossed water. But we leave him and the vision fades;

we return to times when nature is a small environment, tainted
by spills, a deepening wound, fiery in its upheaval, a madness of atoms
in chains of artificial daylight; we walk the beaches crowded now

with a heavier waste, make sounds at the edge of a hollow sea.
This is the legacy we have left ourselves; we are the ones without voices
that cry out as enemies and yet do not say a word; we move through

seas like octopi ink, through trees with hands like blades,
and call for a history that has no plot, in a land without dangers,
without predators. Or those with the teeth to chew seeds,

fish, bones, shells, trees, remnants of speech, spit a glaze, a web
that burnishes the sky. We leave him on the day of his greatest doubt,
    the tides
spewing up foam at his feet, the gulls circling like springs in a watch.

The seals startled by our incessant talk, plunge from the rocks
into the iron glow of that flattened light, and give themselves up
like drops of blood into the sea. And so we see in the loam

our sacrifice. But of what? At the end of our run, at the end

of our reading, we look for him, standing alone at the edge of the world
that falls between us, staring out into the glassy non-existence of things

toward a dead separation, looking for a wind that transforms the sea,
looking for the last heel print in the darkening mouth of the sand,
anything to send us out from the cliffs, out into the fist of storm, to
    breathe.

DREAM POEM ONE

My little brother is in Spain
somewhere along the coast
Cartagena or Gibraltar
at his eternal age
twenty or twenty-one
some fifteen year ago
and under some kind of house
arrest, restricted in his activities:
he cannot hang posters
from his walls, he cannot play
his guitar, or build his wild
antique phones. There is an anti-artistic
regime in power
and my brother has done something
as he does, by doing nothing
and upset those who
decide poetic license.
For some reason, for some
inexplicable undercurrent cause
I will not explore
I know the man in power
or am familiar with him, he's
somehow with me
and in diplomatic form
in my well learned subservient
pose, I ask him why
these insane restrictions.
He is a dark and enigmatic man
thin as someone bound
up in international but voiceless
things, quick to smile
at something deep inside

and quick to change.
He agrees some of these
restrictions seem extreme
there should be no harm
in having inoffensive posters
on an apartment wall
as long as they are deemed
politically neutral
but his eyes change with my pleas
for full release. No
there are good reasons he says
that I can't see. I rush to tell my brother
his art is okay, he can join his friends
in playing music and building
decadent displays of sculpted remains.
His phones. He can come out.
But he is dark himself now
and the anger that was kindled
by first refusal, the thought that any
one would stop him, cut him short
in his personal act, has seeded
deep inside and he cannot shake
the history of his own oppression.
I see it all in passing, the great
waves of political decay
the new order of old men.
He sees the same faces
surrounding him, the same names
forbidden to be spoken
the same silence when he approaches
the same hand on his shoulder
caught in an inescapable age

twenty or twenty-one
and darkened to roots by a stain
that ruins his first and last true acts.
He hears the silence orchestrated
that runs through me like a blade
but for him it is etched with figures
each draining a rivulet of blood
each grooved in the taboo
of his own stain, each hand
lithe and subtle, and the indelible
shadow of my own.

IMAGINARY NIGHTS

Once around a fire in Canada
I listened to the woods open up its throat and breathe
out of the ancient hollow of its torso

and sweep the sparks from the flames
and rotted wood into a murderous column
of suicidal fireflies

lighting on the needles of a mammoth pine
and dying there. I watched time
in a way I have never seen it since

unfold its billowy layers of flesh
and sit before me, the shadow of a tree
and the fire's dimensional light.

The forests were burning and the heat
produced an oven of the landscape
and a charred permanence of single strokes

against the years of first light. I was
the only human form, the only awkwardness
in destruction. I was the only one.

The blackness that followed me was complete
an absolute absence of vegetal distinction
an almost perfect silhouette of natural space.

I did not move and the night
did not end, the fireflies of transformed pine
circled in the air. By morning

the trees were safe, the gray stones
surrounding the firepit were cold and wet
with Canada's inevitable prewinter change.

But the time remained, lingered like death
at the peripheral limits of my senses
and still I move through trees like a spark

through darkness at times, still the woods' throat
chortles, and the fireflies light and for a moment
blaze, and then cool to cinders.

And all but the image of time has changed
and the old climate and the ancient and invisible
terrain has disappeared, and the trees

have grown or died and rotted away. But some nights
still, between the light and the density of trees
I stoke the fire and watch the fireflies ascend.

WOLF FROM THE AIR

Almost a lumbering canter
across the wide snow plain, a long stride
that keeps him low to the ground
and somehow only intermittently
visible, sliding in and out
of his own ground shadow.
On the move, singing to the moon
now only in disguise, not a noise here
but the single engine caught
in glide patterns downward. The first shot
kicks up snow. And then...
he staggers. The hard echo of ice
cracking beneath an empty stretch of plain
unheard from the air.

STONE HOUSE

There is a space within that harbors the sea
as it rushes up to the door of the old stone house
that has been there since my private reckoning.
When as a young man I walked through
the low frame of an absent door
out into the air, the first noticeable thing, half
Scottish, still primal, and Irish, an air of the perpetual sea
that was answer good enough for its time
planted in me as rows of dry seed.
It is a house of hand formed stones
that fit together in a way no one knows of any longer,
a craft that passed into the quickness of long days
and turned walls to impenetrable mysteries.
The house gets older as my year begins
and the sea more distant. I was wandering then
through my own sense of ruins, those slow
rounded hovels in decay, when the sun in its rampage
caught the edge of the upper wall and fired it
like sacrifices against the deepening shift of the sea.
You might have seen, here, the contrast
but it is only the famous unconsciousness of water
moving at the edge of my visible world.
This cast of light and darkness and the ensuing
sense of once again, and sometime out there, again
was enough to tell me the house was more
than an image I harbored and hid from the world.
It is a space that the sea spends itself trying to fill,
a human abode that has lost touch with its bones,
its flesh, and remains a signal to the winds
that inland, here, among the other stones,
unfashioned, formed in a wake of storms or upheavals
in the house, the space I once watched the sea from

as it rushed up to this door
that yet opens out into a sudden madness
of crashing surf, before returning order.

ARCTIC SUN

Like blood rising through ice
to a molten orange
through a molten orange
to the fiery ratification
of a pure and colorless landscape.
From the northern most tip
of the Northwest Territories
the other orb distills
etches the sky.
At horizon where earth rests
and air is solid with the dead cold
of night, the eye, the Other
touches the white plain
captures this dark speck who I am.

BOWEN ISLAND

The rains have let up as we start out
across Howe Sound, the fjord
that looks, for those of us still foreign
to places born of water in such stretches,
as though we might journey northward
for an eternity, into the woodlands
of an unknown Canada.

This day of a rare few
returning to the city of my early dreams
of outwardness, visions while in school
in Oregon of a lasting escape,
the name of the country where humans
worked with the silence of trees
as neighbors, grows calm
like warm air on the water
before the ferry.

Bringhurst, our guide
speaks so very little
that his presence becomes itself a journey
marking the passage as if to some
ancestral home, a returning to the earth
known only on the islands,
an earth of microcosmic intensity
and shy separateness.

He's promised the ruins
of an old colony
of writers. The stone foundation left
of a house that burned, years after
Malcolm Lowry drank and scribbled

passages in its small cold rooms.

But for me, Bowen Island
is a hundred miles north of anywhere,
of any known road to somewhere else,
it tastes of the wilderness in its greenery,
distances itself by the sun
painted in single colored strokes
across its southern shore,
a wild link to my once fervid dream
of living out this time in the close
thicknesses of pure world.

The poet points out the grand chalets
abutted to the passing cliffs
in rows like self-crystallizing blocks of ice,
says he's left the island,
still out a ways before us,
for these reasons:
the noise of hammers
dispersed in the flight of birds;
the frogs disappearing but still,
too many crossing the road.

Where was it I would hide
I think, my mind stretched to the place
like a skin pulled tight over the water.
The fjord I thought was a passage north
curved back around by Keats
Island, and solitude...

    if I must with thee dwell

Let it not be among the jumbled heap
Of murky buildings...

rather here
in a foregone wilderness
of recycled bones;
a crowded death that seeps between
the walls we carve,
as if this were some
rarified dream where at last
we leave the planet.

Entering the small harbor
it seems the town
is pretty much the same
he says, but the street is paved.
It would be best if it rained.
There is a lone frog
somewhere off the path
we stop to hear:
the sound of troubled sleep,
the air, filled with things
we cannot help but breathe.

THE LARGEST ALASKAN YELLOW CEDAR IN THE WORLD

Suddenly, you are alone with the planet
in a universe of comparative sizes,
where the moon is washed out by suns
and the closest stars still lightyears like other lifetimes
distant, unreachable
even in this simply thought.
Then at about five miles in
when the centipede greens of the rainforest
close around you to a thin arch
of parted ferns, and even as you move
the time slips, or has collapsed
into the center of this world
where you turn more slowly than the planet,
you stumble upon an old forestry sign
and a few feet ahead, the ruin
of a giant yellow cedar.

In an instant you are no longer
alone, but crossed by some mania
for markers, the other world's
sign of discovery you think,
or more, a broken half-trunk
of what was once so natural, incomparable,
even among primordial surroundings.
Perhaps some prehistoric wind,
last belch of a dying volcanic age,
when the heat abated
and the cold strength of its northern passage
touched this trunk three flights up
and snapped it in two.

If you were a scientist

you would measure around its base,
tape the rough contours of these roots
connected to the gnarly trunk
in benchlike ridges, map out each
errant growth, each nodule of bark,
a ring or two bulbed out in wetter climes
a hundred years before, fractals
of forgotten environmental change,
but instead you're struck
with the impossibility of exactitude
here, in monstrous dimensions.

Whoever found this apparition
of arboreal genetics
was lucky: here it rests
a few yards from the trail
easily marked. Was it already
some alien, a splintered seed
caught up in an inexhaustible
Alaskan wind, drifting down
through centuries, colder regions,
into Quinault territory?
You stare at the graying remnants,
the ancient broken twig.

And you feel yourself rare
as an extinct orchid in bloom
only once, at the fiery moment
of some volcanic eruption,
and that with a common childhood in Jersey,
years out West, the time in Europe
and in Asia, all to reach this strange point

of greenly kinship, out five miles
from what was nowhere to begin with,
a ranger's shack at road's end;
yet the years between diminished now
by judgments: this,
the largest in the world.

As if no one had been there
you stand in undergrowth of spare instants,
and feel you've seen
a junction of the real world.
When elsewhere, in some less traveled,
untraveled terrain, in a steeper range
where valleys run so deep
the eager pilots have even missed it:
some beast of a tree
perhaps with all its upper limbs
grows without contemplation,
wraps its muscled roots around
the heart of your planet;
and unseen for private centuries,
perhaps for the remainder of this world,
swells, sucks in the land
but dreams of nothing that we might
measure, reaching, without gesture,
toward a small sun.

MEETING BEAR

Over the twelfth ridge
climbing toward an unfurled sky
where the alpine tundra dries
from the rainforest jungle
of ten ridges below;
a mother and her two
full-grown cubs.

It's May and I'm twelve
miles in and alone
on the Olympic Peninsula,
weighted down with a bright red pack
and now frozen to a spot like a tree
as she watches
but the young ones are busy
in the bush
and have not seen me.

For a moment she stops
her world is every twig and leaf
for miles, the snow crusted,
patches up the ridge
toward the rocks at the foot of the sky
and the wind itself does not
change her hearing.

She is great
and black even her eyes
are dark pearls of a forested sea
and her bulk is the muscle
of the hillside she climbs
and her children

are companions now
grown into their own.

I am tired
not just from the miles
up this Olympic set of ridges
in May before the trails
are dry and the snow
is deep as my thigh at times
and yet the sun is extreme.

I am tired
in a new sense
looking at her standing quite still
against the hillside where her
children forage upward
toward barren rock at the edge of sky
and she waits for me
but I cannot make a simple move.

The rank smell
of my own three day clothing
and the forgetfulness of my year
and the trickle of life that bleeds
from my invisible wound
and my body
stands there in her presence
only suddenly aware.

No one might ever know
if we were to merge here on the hillside
in a deadly dance of circles

and howls and the sky
splits open like a melon on stone
and the wind carries our cries
into a thin reed whistle
of voices between needles
of the pines.

For a moment we dance
and the rocks tremble and fall
and the snows melt a little further
into the blueness of the atmosphere
and then the cubs move off
uphill toward bush and rock
and we stand perfectly still
for a moment in two worlds
and then she turns away
and follows.

EUTHANASIA

The western sea spits up its many corpses,
the gulls drop and scavenge through remains,
the painless crabs, the fearless jellyfish.

Along the front range miller moths
in caterpillar states clog the thistleberry and willows
with white gossamer nests of ritual dance,

small jerks of movement as the selves evolve
before the blessing of the cowbirds,
the great dark sweep of insatiable death.

The pain has grown so acute
it transforms the memory, life before blossoms
like a wound inside, the change,

a million years in evolution, a day against
a thousand days, down to the minute
the self is so pure it calls out to dissolve.

Whole populations live in agony, and their fear
corrodes the urban landscape like exhaust
and their dreams rot like clothing washed in acid.

It is not a moral question, a question
of self-determination, the sea consumes its own
and buries them within itself, but

a dream of something else, a poor illusion
of the way things ought to be, surely, proven,
the way life was meant to carry us without effect.

If you watch your pain it grows,
if you wish beyond it it curls back into your present
and strikes like a venomous wish.

We have lost the art of death, the day,
each day, against all others, each one the last
opening like a troubled birth,

each death a means of seeing life, a staying
of remains, a transformation but not from
who we never were;

more, a movement that completes what we
want, the end of desire, the pure
refusal to submit. In darkness light

situates us, not some heavenly hope,
not some long awaited moment of release
but a body moving through an endless space

toward an understanding of it,
a taste of time that finally leaves that time
somewhere behind it, a sea

that in its rhythms refuses to save
its tumultuous breeds, each washed up
and retrieved, taken back to where

there is no other place to go.
The escape is our illusion, the swimming
makes us dizzy with its false procession.

ANTARCTIC

White without cause, celestial network
of footprints, earth bowl,
wind chime of tonelessness, absence of sleep
and sleep of objects, frozen time
and the clicks of time, space of centuries,
robe of perfect blindness,
walls of sky, disappearing wound of horizon,
let me rest here
in the impossible absence of color,
in the rudiments of all lands, the purity of two elements,
wind and water, and earth like a rumor,
and sunlight like the taste of distant fire,
let me stand against the land
as shadow, as visitant without true reason,
enveloped in the whirlwind of moments
without the weight of definition.

For the stretches beyond the wolves,
beyond the last gnarled remnants of ancient pine,
out at the edge of a curve that contains
all inanimate things within its sphere,
all angles of wood and stone, all microscopic worlds,
for the last measurement,
the last possible thought of return,
are all part of my need here,
part of the sanctity of nothingness in white,
a song of low winds across a featureless terrain.
The land is the ancestor of these eyes,
the buried ground of my blood
and its torrents. It is here I would merge
with the forgotten fires of this cold planet
where the land I am is offered up
in the teeth of the sky.

PASSAGE TO YELLOWSTONE

From way up north, beyond the false border,
down from Banff, or further, from north of Jasper,
for some unknown reason, not reason
but *in naturam,*
the wolf follows a thin and ancient scent trail
through the workings of a fragmented world.
Down the Waterton and Glacier
down the Flathead Range,
each year a little further, moving
and denning, always moving
but in wide arcs of untracked wilderness
now bordered on the edge of us,
those who have a history
of their destruction.

The cattle stand like monuments
to sloth, the slow and retarded movements
of the grain-fed, the constancy of eating
like a station in life, eating
the sun as it ventures down
and sinks beneath the open field.

The wary pace, the eyes
always in the distance, penetrating the trees
envisioning what? The sense of wind
that races up a valley some ridges off?
The movement of the land.

After a century of relentless death,
the slow and gradual return.
The cycle of something unknown for those of us
who see our end in straight progressions,

our end in ourselves. The wolf
ranges south into our segmented world
perhaps to see what has changed,
perhaps because the scent has not faded,
is still strong in the markings on new trees.
Perhaps because the wolf cannot live
but by the power of its needs,
the rumor that its past is still here lingering,
that its memory is mixed with ours,
sending us a shred of old fear
that we must do it again, cut off the passage
to our other selves.

SATURDAY NIGHT DANCE AT BORING HIGH

The girls have waited their whole lives for this
one weekend. The dresses are pressed and spread
across the satin covers on the canopied beds
and the sun hangs on the sky's edge
like a neighborhood boy, a youthful despoiler.

I enter the town by its roots
through the old growth forest at its edge
and sit among the still wet camouflage
of its antiquity. The boys are out
cruising by early dusk and dreaming of steel

and armor, whispering between
the murmur of their engines across gulfs
of wet silence reflected off the pavement of the streets.
Lightening transforms the sky
at the crease where the clouds perpetuate

a sleepy insistence, a slow retrieval of needs
from an outer world that has gone unwired.
It is easy to see this true infusion of sleep
as reorder, retreat, but the boys
purr past in a slow procession of darkening ardor

and harbored schemes. Their world rolls
down the main at my feet, curves
toward an endless juncture of sky and giant trees
where the wind cannot move and the rain
makes a passages from leaf to leaf

to reach the decay of the forest floor. The slow
and then sudden ending of the week brings revelations

and mothers stare out fogged windows
into the ancient reflection of the forest. I see
this distillation of dreams, a wet and fervid tangle

of trees, turn to bodies moving across a floor
which creaks and heaves as its joints ring
and its voices slip into the night. The girls
have waited years for this one moment of freedom
from the old growth, from the slow and steady

addition of rings, from the tumbled dead
and the hunger of ferns. They feel the taffeta
of their skirts, brush their hair, settling
quietly on the vinyl seats, and stare out

fogged windows at the endless stream of cars
that disappear into the mirror of vanishing streets
toward the school. In a second, the town winks
and I drive through the center of its eye
myself asleep, lingering on the thought of these

lives insulated by a knot of living green,
living out their night on the edge of things
while others wonder what happens, here
in the rural enclaves, in the towns that seem to sleep
as an ancient hunger eats its ways through the trees.

THE AMERICAN WEST

Nevada. The forbidden planet. The lost desert
with snowcapped peaks that no one since Fremont
possibly has seen. I traverse the Great Basin
on my wanderer's way toward the Northwest,
seeking out a place in myself that echoes with the old
and more vacant land. I am cutting the thin, sinewy
wires of the city, of the folks that crowd around it,
making it vibrant and alive. I would find
the last road built by Eisenhower for national defense,
the last corner of the desert that laughs back
for it is without corners; it is a room of sand
with walls fashioned only out of a fear in seeing
too much. I drive up through the Toiyabe
and Toquima toward the north, through Winnemucca
and out, spreading like a wind without corridors
to guide its voraciousness, out into the Black Rock
Desert, into one of the last empty spaces of this life.

PINES AT THE EDGE OF THE WORLD

Much in nature confuses me:
the insoluble earth, its slow groans toward
short, violent eruption, circles left in still water.

At the edge of one world
as I look out into the fogged light of another
I question this finality,

the sense of passage that pushes at my back and plays fingers
along the moist sand. Here the pines
wait for the seas that pray to their roots

to carry them off, carve their spines
with knives of salt, throw them up again as runes
for the traveler, whose life has been but a moment in their art.

There is something human about these trees
but is that enough? I walk down along the shore
toward Terra del Fuego, toward the cold tip of the planet's last arm

although I am on the Olympic Peninsula
staring at a image of bodies scattered to the south.
Trees speak nothing, they take disease

and die as a single gesture toward some rudimentary transformation,
some unknown sacrifice, but this is ours,
what we put here, how we taste the air from Antarctica

even in a chilled Northwestern breeze.
I look for the dead among the dunes that mimic the ocean's ferocity
in obscurant waves, for the pines that dry to burnished ornaments,

for the symphony of changes that no one hears.
But then no one gathers at the edge of this world at dusk to count
the bodies, the burial trains that rise up with the tides.

We are surely human here, being on the coast
stops nothing of the madness of ourselves as inlanders and boundariless
     peoples,
but it fuses me with its thick particled air, it sings

through drum beats like a savage act of one tone concentration.
And the others who might have been here
have left their marks too close to the edge of this rage,

too sure that the sands that washes out will return
in finer soups of pulverized remains. So the pines play out a dance,
shift listlessly on the disintegrating shore

and mock the way we walk here and leave
as if the land was ours to bury ourselves within
and not a moment of hardened flight that has risen up to hold us at this
     edge.

GHOST DEER

Dumb ghosts of old inhibitions,
soft eyed, indulgent
of the sacred space between us,

gray letters
of subtle indecisions
to walk off, stifflegged
into other lives, at a slow pace
dissolving
as dust in the taboos of rain.

Half a million
slaughtered on our mad web of free
ways—and still they come
down to the water's edge
in artificial light. Not

deaths but metempsychosis;
the thick sleepy lives of our selves
as children, both frozen
in expectation

from a distance
across the open that is marked
by traces of bullets
two hundred years old

embedded in their bones,
but they do not move.
But we could not
turn away.

Now in the headlights
we see our own fear,
some racial memory of night,
some sign glyphed in the clay of our skulls,
the splitting of the total darkness,
the sudden intrusive vision,
edges of the otherness
blurred to outer unconsciousness.

Deer
now inhabit the gaps left
in our cultivation,
in the pure design of streets
linking suburban organs
in thin skeletal frames
like hungry rats.

These are the fleshy
petroglyphs of another's inner tension,
the animal totems of a season
that watch us decay.

Globe eyed
and thick as meat bled dry
the graynesses move
about us. Stare,
locked in a grid of losses,
reach up your hand,
touch the air that once burned
but is cool now,
see how the head turns.

ARCTIC DAY

What can be said about whiteness
has been said, the indefiniteness
of the land, sastrugi and small drifts
like microscopic waves along ridges
smoothed to level by the building snow
washed in shadowless reflection
on which I stand. To walk here
makes it all seem suspended
from any sense of distance, there is
no going anywhere, even by plane
the land becomes a spaceless surface
where everything you think
remains the same, one thing, and caught
on it, I'm unable to read my death.

HORSES

for Sarah H.

They rise up from the far side of the bluff
against the turquoise sky in diffused light
like a fiery brigade or pack of long range wolves

but heavily, each movement in a flow of muscled sea
syncopated, like fingers in a slow crescendo
down the evening keys of dust and wild wheat.

They circle left without a single brush
of flank or mane, and drop below the bluff's far edge
to rise again against the submerging sun.

It is impossible to see which one
is gray, which brown or gold, for the flow
of shades is a movement of the earth itself

of rock and brush, of dust and green
dissolving light. This change, the wind
perhaps, or the stones beneath them cooling down

and the lead stallion turns his head
to see you, standing where the open prairie
gives you no cover. So suddenly, there and alone

and almost invisibly, in the very same terrain,
an arm's length in your mind
from the sweating sides and scattered manes,

from the rush of hooves and nostrils. You feel
the wind sweep through the grasses all around you
as if you too were running, high

above the bluff on that pulse of wild rushing flood
that merges with your senses, sight and sound,
one hand wrapped tight in coils of ragged mane

as the sun drops down, and you sense the others
turning, out toward the high lines of a snowy range,
you disappear in clouds of trailing particles of sun.

WOLF-CROSS KILLS CHILD

In any other neighborhood
the moon was drinking milk from the cup of the sky
and the sun had not yet set. But here the half-dog
moves restless at the end of his tether
in a chained circle beneath the red of sun half filtered
through the dusk particles in the air, at obtuse angles
to the cooling earth. A child's scream is like
a hawk's, it sends out reverberations through the trees,
marks the point of its body against time
but without knowing it. No one is home
at the crucial hours in this neighborhood
when the solar forces change place, when the light moves
into its altering states. The world is empty
but for the movements that have remained unchanged
for millennium. No one, the papers say,
is to blame.

In the growing darkness the eyes
become a medium of exchange. The new light is like
water to sea creatures, an envelope of second skin,
an outer lung wrapping the breath within the furred
and lonely senses. All movement is either enemy
or kin, either the spheres in slow progression
or the spirits outside. Then there is always
the halt at the end, the stiff jerk of chain at the neck,
the world cut short, closed in. The moon,
a partner, moves off alone among the trees
and the sun dissolves. In time, the senses all are full
like muscles twitching in sleep, sights and sounds
crowd into the circle of the world
like fists or missiles, like sudden moments when the earth
disappears and the animal is surrounded. There is

something more primal between the senses
these two share, a raw nerve of coming night
exposed to the oldest of ways.

At dusk the world is thick with its own remains;
it reaches into the neighborhood with
moistened tongue. One sphere moves where
the other has not yet waned, for a moment
the sun sees what it gives light to each night,
is shocked by the suddenness of its own white gaze
and the blood of evening is its ritual of exchange.
The instincts sleep, but wake at a slow,
shifting of the night, encroach on the living like fire
runs through those same trees, a kindling
of dry urbanity, a stripping away. It is not
a question of on what the world feeds, the stilled
senses, the appetites embedded at birth increased
by dull age. Day lends itself to night, night
always remains. The cry is a cross on the night,
a calling of moons, a howling at something almost there
that has suddenly slipped away.

NEAH BAY

For its part, this passage north
ends in the fist of land that juts into the Straits
of Juan de Fuca, on a peninsula itself
a fist, a dark heart of enormous trees.

The Makah go about their business,
disappearing, no one stays at home, here
in the neighborhood of the sea, but takes a chance
inland, outside the tribe.

The young man at the museum says
the feds determine our Indianness by degrees
of which we are slowly depleted, intermingling
with worlds of otherness. "One day

we will no longer exist, our bloodlines
run so thin that the government will not see us..."
and the sea will devour these shores.
Today, also lost, I see only a tongue of land

tied to currents on three sides, the fishing trollers
in need of paint, or a good season, lulled
in their slips, soft repetitions, anchored
to a few blocks of half-paved streets.

The violence within me, the rage of self
like surf, salt fierceness of unchecked eruptions,
an untempered tug of moon and sun, frenzied
and riotous, a sudden wash of who this is

standing on the land. "If I had one wish,"
he says, "I'd make each of us stay right where we are

for two hundred years." To live, I think, what's left
behind, to inherit what we cannot escape.

PETROLEUM CREEK

For fourteen miles I dream the sound of water over rocks
entering the sea, along the coastal strip of uncharted sands
that wash up against the cliffs and pool in pockets of volcanic ash
hardened into deep ravines and microscopic seas,

but the water that greets me, spreads out across the sands,
sucked up by the waiting currents of the surf
like a dog's tongue lapping the surface of a shallow indentation,
is the color of oil, the seepage of the deeper rusted land.

By the totality of salt air and sea, the complete body of the other,
not birthplace or habitat, but a distant flatness ruffled with undercurrent,
fingertips of some other sense of life than this,
there is no water to drink, no savior but the oil of the angered land.

Crouching by the creek I filter out a thermos half full of dark,
undistilled blood, the last dregs of the spring, the wash
of tarnished stones. And from this vantage point look west
to the drainage of this meager runoff into the body of its other self,

the sudden crash of a cresting wave, the hunger of the sea,
to realize the difference in this living stuff, this evolutionary end,
that makes its common past a world apart, unmemoried,
the disproportioned cradle of a voice, cut loose by primal thirst.

SINGLETRACK

Why the wolf shadows us
in his solitary lope toward a dark cul de sac
of pine, across the dim, white plain
I can't say. But he does. He moves out
at an angle to the moon on legs
taunt as limbs of a twisted wood,
knowing only direction, seeing
the whole landscape as a matrix
of sights and sounds and smells.
Why I pick this beast, my dog,
more wolf than husky, halfbreed, to say
these things, more human than human,
more watchful than those who watch,
more singleminded than I can ever
hope to be, remains a mystery of some
complexity, a human instance
of chaos, a wish fulfilled by sight alone,
no involvement. I know
there are indigenes that identify
with this slow lope,
with the eye as yellow-orange
as a ground haze-cradled sun,
with the sense of all senses
at once, the madness of knowing
too much of what goes on around him.
But I choose the wolf for more
than this, for his direct line
through life to death,
for the immediacy of his fear
of people, his sense that there is no
custom, no acquaintanceship
that suffices to remove the terror

of one's own species
or of the other. He appears here
for his lope through powdered snow,
the single line that connects him
to nowhere, a notion
he would be comfortable with if
comfort were a notion to him. No,
connected more to the whole
white plain, to the way the sun
hands down the sky
to the hillside, to the way
the wind tastes the dead wheat weeds
frozen to their necks. There are ways
of saying humans move, but then
they change, and we adapt
perhaps, to this, or not, but change
the ways we move nonetheless.
This dog part wolf changes
as an act of nature, drifts through
his selves like water curled
by the tail of a trout, stays the same
as current, curves off of rocks
and continues. His senses
are not a reaching out but a hollow
where the light and air slow
to hover, an indentation
in the landscape of his own
mixed presence. His customs
are discrete, his sense of others
real, and his movements
always out and away,
far enough to turn and see

what follows, who wants
more than a stare,
more than sharing the same
hillside a mile away.
This is why I watch the wolf
as I can, follow his singletrack
when his fear of people
takes him up, when he disappears.
I grant humans their due,
this word for one, the sight
that stays after the wolf has gone,
but his is a unsensed vision,
a touch of worlds on all fronts,
a skin of earth and sky and
a rumor in his blood.
His lies are never false moves
but simply changes of direction,
his symbol is the singletrack
he makes, traversing
what remains, a narrow habitat,
the place he knows
that can never close him in.

THE INVISIBLE MAN

He rides an elevator to work
in a city that is constantly burning

carries his heart in a briefcase that is leather
pure and simple in black and gold

walks without a movement of the head
or arms like a forgotten gesture

only the legs retain
slides his chair out as silently

as death in the street below
at a crosswalk at an odd corner

at a faulty stoplight
a slippage or a clog or a cough

that spasms, a fog of breath against the sky
the noise of it absorbed into canyons

of glass vistas like his own
into antlike gestures swirling

into pockets of brief concern
he walks back to his chair

faces the day in paper
falls into the sensible way

and wears, though dead these thirty years
my father's name

an invisible cry into the air
a moment when these faces look the same

THE ZHIVAGO WOLVES

In *Zhivago*
the wolves come at night
and in the middle of the poem.

The winter is their body
and they are mimed by the fur
of those in the summer palace.

We are wrong to think
they fear Yuri's sudden movements.
They are shy of things that change.

They're not an interruption;
when he returns to his desk of ice
he carries their vigilance to his love.

IN THE SPIRIT OF THINGS

When my ancestors, the Celts,
cast their precious metalwork into the river
it was an offering

to more than the river god,
it was a blessing of connectedness
among all elements;

and the riverine deities
rose up, perhaps
into a darkening and angry sky.

From the Thames
retrieved, the Battersea Shield,
the Waterloo Helmet,

and myriad coins;
and today, children on the mall
drop pennies into a murky fountain.

Marne, mother,
from *Matrona* and others,
Verbeia of the River Wharfe and Sabrina,

and closer to my ancestral home,
Boann of the Boyne.
Panpsychism rises

as objects take on life
or as life is object, divided
and moving through the world

like blood through the veins.
Royce said *Where*
we see inorganic Nature

seemingly dead, there is in fact
conscious life,
if there is being in nature at all,

if there is sense of stone in stone.
And now with physics:
we live in an old chaos of the sun,

a hylozoism,
where rather than inert
the world pulses as it turns,

like Gaia, or the local
godlings tied to like geographies
in the landscapes of the Rhine,

or Sequana over the Seine,
Nemausicae at Nimes,
or something even closer

to the pantheism
of the Vedanta
where Brahman is undefined.

But in the fountain
greenish coins
leave circles on the fiberglass.

Elsewhere, spirits rise with dust
through the horse tracks
of a networked West;

or sewers overrun the sea
and the seas run
like wounds with tons of steel.

The blood of this river
empties around my feet
into a different void

and staring out
from the river mouth that touches
a fierce Pacific

it seems the voices
are only hollow sounds
made by the cavern music

of the skull. And the sea—
the sea is an atavistic body,
unconscious yet complete.

ARCTIC MOON

Now the eyes play games
with the land, a pearllike glow
that polishes the senses
with a slowness of breath
and a face that seems so close
I might kiss it. It's as if
the earth here had made its deal
that this was the perfect light
for their collaboration, a trade
of strengths and weaknesses
through this shining edge
to the darkness. Of neither
one nor the other, I want to be
this light, this cold, perfectly fused.

ABOUT THE AUTHOR

George B. Moore's first book of poems, *The Long Way Around,* appeared in 1992. He received a Colorado Council on the Arts COvisions Recognition Award for Literature in 1996, and has been a finalist for the National Poetry Series, the Brittingham Poetry Award and the Anhinga Poetry Prize. He lives with his friend, Tayo, a wolf-hybrid, in Boulder, Colorado, where he teaches literature and writing at the University of Colorado.

Photo by Gary Kinchner